Toy Models

Written by Margie Burton, Cathy French, and Tammy Jones

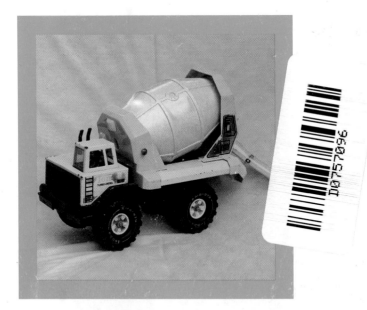

A car is a toy.

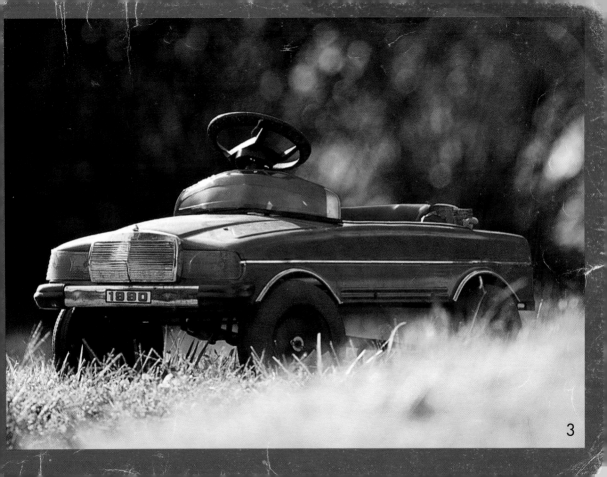

A boat is a toy.

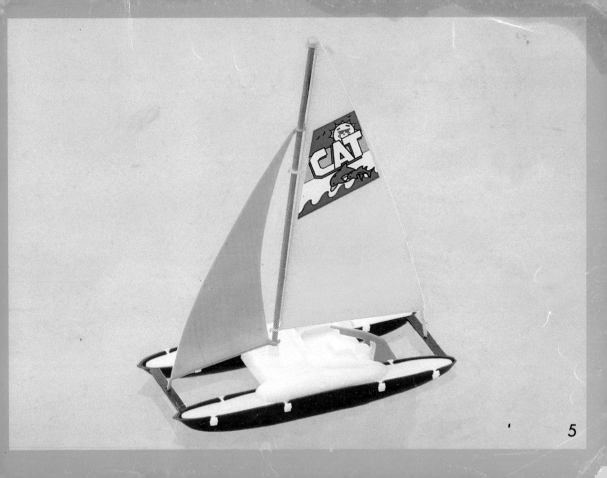

5

A truck is a toy.

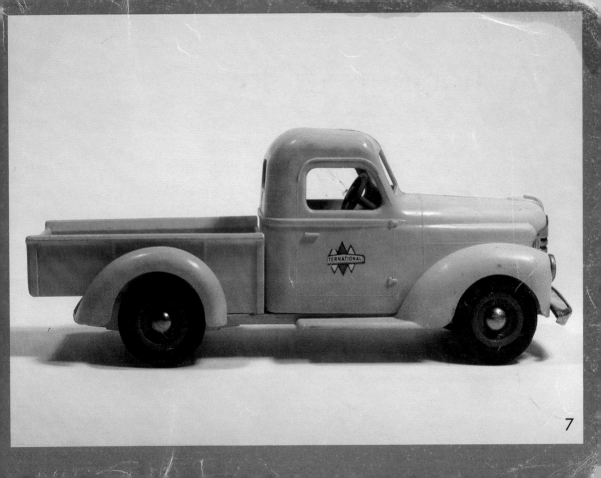

A horse is a toy.

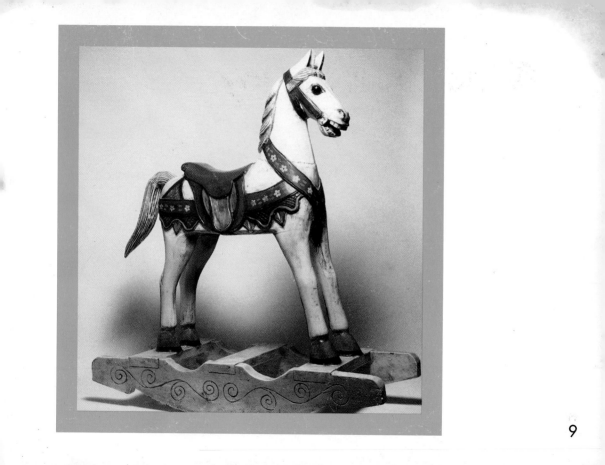

A doll is a toy.

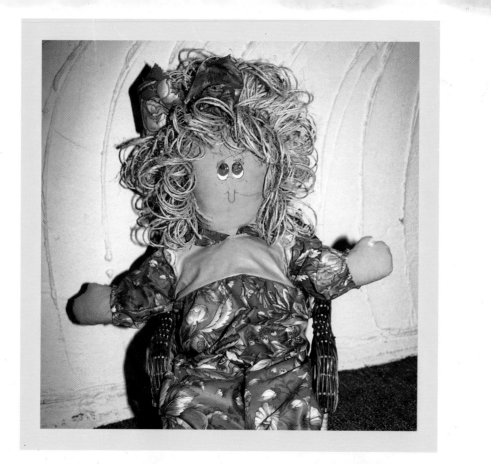

11

A farm is a toy.

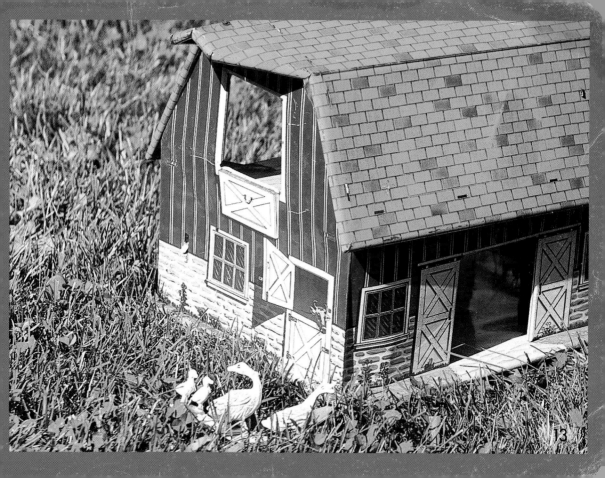

A train is a toy.

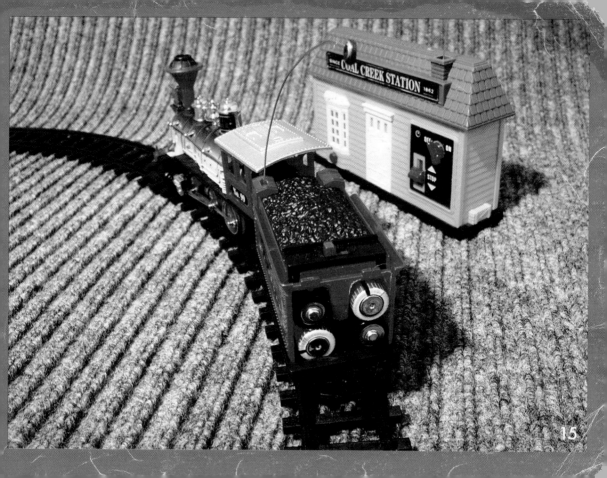

A house is a toy.

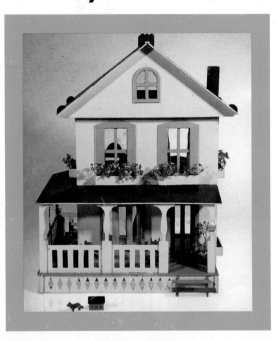